Find Your Way!

Move to the head of the class with geography puzzles to help you pass!

by Kristi Thom

⭐ American Girl®

Questions or comments? Call 1-800-845-0005, visit **americangirl.com,** or write to Customer Service, American Girl, 8400 Fairway Place, Middleton, WI 53562-0497.

Printed in China
12 13 14 15 16 17 18 19 LEO 10 9 8 7 6 5 4 3 2 1

Editorial Development: Trula Magruder
Art Direction and Design: Camela Decaire
Production: Jeannette Bailey, Kendra Schluter, Meagan Eggers, Tami Kepler, Judith Lary
Illustrations: Thu Thai at Arcana Studios

Dear Reader,

Welcome to Innerstar University! At this imaginary, one-of-a-kind school, you can live with your friends in a dorm called Brightstar House and find lots of fun ways to let your true talents shine.

One of your talents might be a flair for geography. To find out, follow your guide, Paige, as she takes you on a puzzle journey across campus, through the United States, and around the world. Using your geography skills and Paige's tips, see if you can solve the puzzles, brainteasers, and mazes inside. Not only will you learn about capitals, continents, maps, and more, but you'll also get to know what Innerstar U and its students are like.

If you get stuck or just want to check your answers, turn to page 72. Have a good time finding your way through all the puzzles! Then head over to www.innerstarU.com for even more fun and games.

Your friends at American Girl

Innerstar Guides

Every girl needs a few good friends to help find her way.
These are the friends who are always there for you.

Emmy

A brave girl who loves swimming and boating

Isabel

A confident girl with a funky sense of style

Riley

A good sport, on the field and off

Paige

A nature lover who leads hikes and campus cleanups

Amber

An animal lover and a
loyal friend

Neely

A creative girl who loves
dance, music, and art

Logan

A super-smart girl
who is curious about
EVERYTHING

Shelby

A kind girl who is there
for her friends—and loves
making NEW friends!

Innerstar U Campus

1. Rising Star Stables
2. Star Student Center
3. Brightstar House
4. Starlight Library
5. Sparkle Studios
6. Blue Sky Nature Center

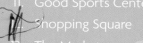

Table of Contents

Check it out, and then check it off!

All Around Innerstar University

The Great United States

What a World!

Answers start on page 72.

Meet Paige

Work side by side with your Innerstar University guide.

At Innerstar University, Paige is the campus explorer. She loves hiking, nature, and taking care of the world.

Because of Paige's enthusiasm for maps, geography, and the environment, she's the perfect guide to lead you through this book—she might even slow you down to observe the unique places she knows around campus!

Paige has a passion for exploring the unknown—either by studying maps, walking nature paths, or traveling to other countries. That's why she wants you to discover how amazing it is to learn about places and spaces beyond your front door. Who knows? You might find that you love geography, too!

Look for my speech bubbles for tips and guidance throughout this book.

INNERSTAR UNIVERSITY

All Around
Innerstar
University

Direction Detection

Paige knows a little saying to help her remember where north, east, south, and west are on the compass. To decode her saying, solve the clues, and then read your answers from top to bottom.

The opposite of always:

N __ __ __ __

When you chew food and swallow it, you

E __ __

When something gets wet and drippy, it's

S __ __ __ __

A breakfast food like pancakes with squares on them:

W __ __ __ __ __ __

Busy Day

Today Paige has a l-o-n-g list of activities she'd like to do but not enough time to do them all. To get in as many as she can, she's decided to choose the place nearest her dorm in each time slot. Pull out the ISU map from the back of this book, and circle the activity that's closest to Brightstar House in each time slot.

(8 A.M.) Take a riding lesson at Rising Star Stables.
Return a book to Starlight Library.

(10 A.M.) Make a craft at Sparkle Studios.
Catch a game at Good Sports Center.

(12 P.M.) Kayak at Starfire Lake & Boathouse.
Visit Blue Sky Nature Center.

(2 P.M.) Fly kites at Morningstar Meadow.
Do yoga at Real Spirit Center.

(4 P.M.) Study at Star Student Center.
Browse at Shopping Square.

Campus by Compass

Riley left a note for Paige. Pull out your Innerstar U campus map and the compass in the back of this book, and match north on the map with north on your compass. Then carefully read the note to figure out where Paige should meet Riley.

Hi, Paige!
Here's a game I think you'll like. Grab your compass, and follow the directions. I'll meet you at 3:00!
Riley

- Start at 2:30 in front of Brightstar House.
- Walk NE and cross the bridge.
- Turn NW and follow the path.
- Continue across the bridge.
- When the path comes to a T, turn E, and go up the stairs.
- Continue walking until the path comes to a T.
- Turn NW and go across the bridge.
- Walk a short distance and turn E.
- Walk until you come to the bridge. Cross it and turn E.
- There will be a building to the NE. Pass in front of it and walk S down the stairs.
- At the bottom of the stairs, walk E.
- When you come to the star, walk to the NE point.
- Go up the stairs and keep walking. You'll see me ahead!

Where is Paige meeting Riley?

When reading a compass, you need to know north, south, east, and west. These are the cardinal, or main, points on a compass. Midway between the cardinal points are four other points—northwest, northeast, southwest, and southeast.

INNERSTAR UNIVERSITY

Symbol Search

Paige made a fun puzzle for her friends, using a few colorful symbols from her map key. To get from Start to Finish, the friends can move only *left, right, up,* and *down* onto a symbol that has the *same shape* or *same color.* Can you help? We've done a couple of steps for you.

Map Key

 Muddy area

 Bridge

 Wildflower patch

 Steep hill

Maps use symbols (little drawings) so that people can quickly identify specific places and things. Symbols can change from map to map, so most symbols are explained in a map key or legend. Reading maps is kind of like reading a secret code!

Start

Finish

Compass Clues

Paige likes to practice her directions using her compass and the sun. See if you can work your way through her brainteaser list— the problems get harder as you go! Hint: Remember that the sun rises in the east and sets in the west.

1. It's 9:00 in the morning, and you're looking toward the sun. Which way are you facing?

_____

2. You're walking the opposite of south. Which way are you going?

_____

3. You're riding your scooter north, and you turn left. In which direction are you heading now?

_____

4. It's 4:00 in the afternoon, and the sun is behind you. Which way are you facing?

_____

5. You're riding your bike west, and then you turn left. Which way are you riding?

_____

6. You're running south, you turn right, and then you turn right again. Which way are you running?

_____

Like a Hike?

Paige plans to hike with a couple of friends from Blue Sky Nature Center to Camp Innerstar U. She's using the map on pages 20–21. Look closely at the key and the map. Then see if you can help Paige find the easiest trail to hike on.

Key

Steep hill

Mud

Scenic spot

Wildflower patch

Waterfall

Picnic spot

Fallen tree

Bridge

Rocky path

Skunk crossing

Which trail would be the easiest for hikers?

NATURE
HIKE

THIS WEEKEND

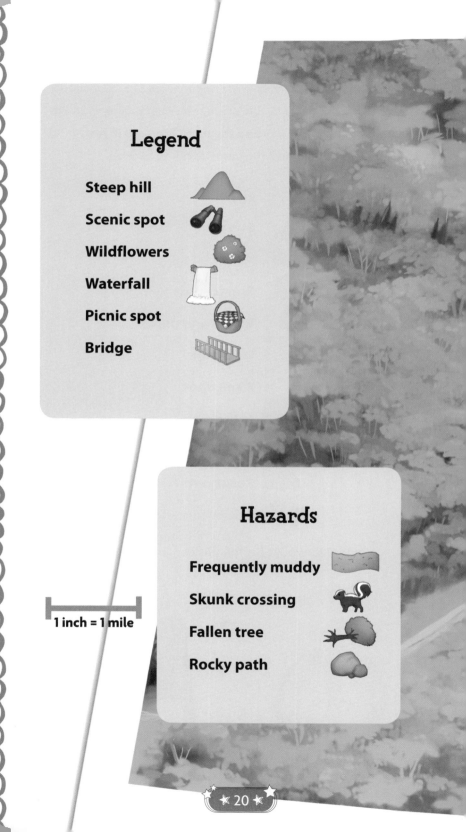

Legend

Steep hill

Scenic spot

Wildflowers

Waterfall

Picnic spot

Bridge

Hazards

Frequently muddy

Skunk crossing

Fallen tree

Rocky path

1 inch = 1 mile

Camp Innerstar U

Hidden Hills Trail

Blue Sky Trail

Starfire Stream

Blue Sky Nature Center

How Far?

Now that Paige has chosen a trail, she wants to figure out how far her friends are going to hike. Use the map on pages 20–21. The scale is one inch equals one mile. That means if the distance between two places on the map is two inches, they're two miles apart. Use a one-inch piece of string or a ruler to help Paige answer the questions below.

1. How far would it be to hike from the first fork in the road near Blue Sky Nature Center to the tent entrance at Camp Innerstar U, using Blue Sky Trail?

2. How far would it be to hike along the path from the tent at Camp Innerstar U to the waterfall and back?

3. How far is it between the two bridges on Hidden Hills Trail?

Scavenger Hunt

The girls of Brightstar House have hidden a birthday surprise for Isabel. Paige left Isabel a compass and hid some clues around her room. To help her find the gift, position your compass from the back of the book so that north lines up with north on Isabel's wall, shown on the following pages.

What is Isabel's gift? ....

Turn left. Sit in the desk chair. If the desk were a clock, the clue would be under 10:00.

Go downstairs. Face E. Look for a clue behind a peaceful spot.

Head straight E. When you see your twin, look down. Your final clue is there.

Head NW to the stairs. Climb the stairs to the bed. Look for the next clue pinned to the E pillow.

Start here!

Isabel, start at the door in your room, and then head SW. Look for clue 2 under the first book you see.

Turn so you're facing S. Hold out your right arm. Head where your hand is pointing until you see a window—and another clue.

N

Go NW to a smaller space, and look on the table. Your gift is there!

An A-maze-ing Day

Paige designed a lawn maze for her friends and left them hints if they happened to go in the wrong directions. Read the clues at right to help the friends make it through the maze.

Start

Pile of acorns:
head back north

Pile of sticks:
head back south

Pile of rocks:
head back east

Pile of leaves:
head back west

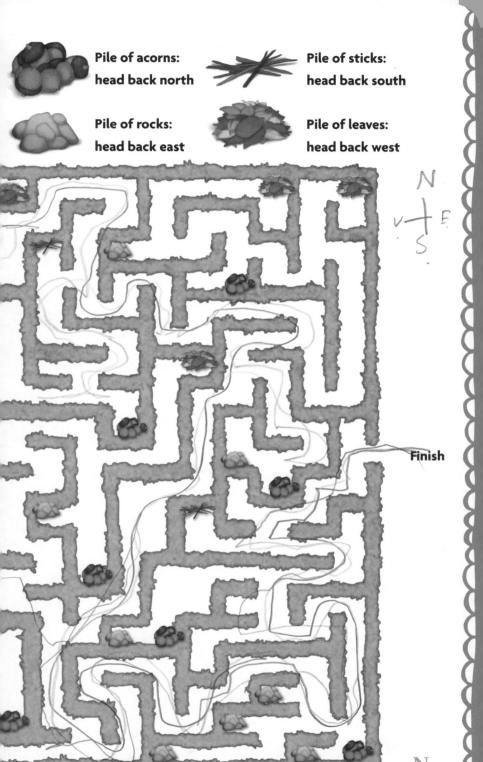

Finish

Itsy-Bitsy Brainteaser

At lunch one day, Paige asked her friends this brainteaser:

There are four words on a compass that name the different directions. Which one of those words does not appear in the names of any states?

The Great
United States

States with Space

A _ A _ A _ A

A _ A _ _ A

A _ I _ _ _ A

A _ _ A _ _ A S

C A _ I _ _ _ _ I A

C _ _ _ _ A _ O

C _ _ _ _ _ _ _ I _ _ T

D _ _ A _ A _ E

F _ _ _ I _ A

G _ _ _ _ I A

H A _ A I I

I _ A _ O

I _ _ I _ _ I S

I _ _ I A _ A

I _ _ A

K A _ _ A S

K _ _ _ _ _ _ _ Y

L _ _ I _ I A _ A

M A I _ E

M A _ _ _ A _ D

M A _ _ A _ _ _ _ _ _ _ S

M I _ _ I _ A N

M I _ _ _ _ _ _ _ A

M I _ _ I _ _ I _ _ I

M I _ _ _ _ _ _ I

M _ _ _ A _ A

N _ _ _ A _ _ A

N _ _ A _ A

N _ _ _ A _ _ _ _ I _ E

N _ _ _ _ _ _ _ _ Y

Paige has tried to memorize the names of all of the states in alphabetical order. Just for fun, see how many you can fill in. We've added the first and last letters, plus all the A's and I's.

N _ _   _ _ _ I _ O

N _ _   _ _ _ K

N _ _ _ _   C A _ _ _ I _ A

N _ _ _ _   _ A _ _ _ A

O _ I O

O _ _ A _ _ _ A

O _ _ _ _ N

P _ _ _ _ _ _ _ A _ I A

R _ _ _ _ _   I _ _ A _ D

_ _ _ _ _   _ A _ _ _ I _ A

S _ _ _ _   _ A _ _ _ A

T _ _ _ _ _ _ _ E

T _ _ A S

U _ A H

V _ _ _ _ _ _ T

V I _ _ I _ I A

W A _ _ I _ _ _ _ N

W _ _ _   _ I _ _ I _ I A

W I _ _ _ _ _ _ I N

W _ _ _ I _ G

Quarter Quiz

Paige was looking at her state-quarter collection and noticed that four of her quarters have horses on them and four have boats. Read about each state, and see if you can match the state to its quarter.

Delaware:
This quarter shows a man riding 80 miles to cast a deciding vote for America's independence from England.

Kentucky:
This quarter shows a thoroughbred racehorse in a state famous for its racehorses.

Nevada:
This state has many wild horses.

Wyoming:
This state has cowboys and rodeos.

A _____

B _____

C _____

D _____

E ....

F ....

G ....

H ....

New Jersey:
This quarter shows America's first president
crossing a river in a boat.

Virginia:
This quarter shows America's first English colonists
arriving on sailing vessels.

Rhode Island:
A sailing boat is appropriate for this state since about
30 percent of its total area is water.

Missouri:
On this state quarter, Lewis and Clark are
floating down the Missouri River.

Map Mistakes

Paige is working on a unique map of the United States.
Just for fun, she put 20 crazy mistakes in it to see if her friends
could find them all. List below the ones you find. If you get stuck,
compare her poster to the real map on page 37.

Extra credit: I've
removed one of the
U.S.'s favorite states
from my map. Can you
see which one?

PAIGE'S MAP
OF THE
UNITED STATES

What's In Common?

A group of students, talking before their geography class, discovered that the names of their home states have something in common. Can you figure out what it is?

The states they are from:

Connecticut
Hawaii
Illinois
Massachusetts
Minnesota

Mississippi
Missouri
Pennsylvania
Tennessee

More In Common

Later on, another group of students looking at a map of the United States realized that the states they were all from had something in common. Look at the map and see if you can figure out what it is!

The states they were from:

Alaska—AK

Arizona—AZ

California—CA

Idaho—ID

Maine—ME

Michigan—MI

Minnesota—MN

Montana—MT

New Hampshire—NH

New Mexico—NM

New York—NY

North Dakota—ND

Texas—TX

Vermont—VT

Washington—WA

Even More In Common

Then the girls from Utah, Wyoming, Colorado, and New Mexico realized that their home states had something in common. Look at the states, and see if you can figure out what it is.

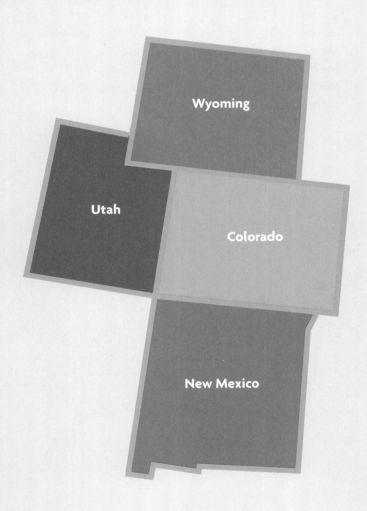

Still More In Common

Paige said to Isabel, "My aunt lives in a state that looks like a mitten." Isabel said, "That's funny, because my aunt lives in a state that looks like a glove!" Paige said, "Hey, that means our aunts are neighbors!"

Look at your US map on page 37, and use your imagination to find the neighboring states that look a little like a mitten and a glove. What two states are these girls' aunts from?

.... and ....

Souvenir Scramble

Each region of the US is represented by a collection of similar souvenirs. Look closely at the collection, and then write the names of each state in the correct list below.

The West: Pencils

1. ....
2. ....
3. ....
4. ....
5. ....
6. ....
7. ....
8. ....
9. ....
10. ....
11. ....
12. ....
13. ....

The South: Spoons

1. ....
2. ....
3. ....
4. ....
5. ....
6. ....
7. ....
8. ....
9. ....
10. ....
11. ....
12. ....
13. ....
14. ....
15. ....
16. ....

The Midwest: Mugs

1. ....
2. ....
3. ....
4. ....
5. ....
6. ....
7. ....
8. ....
9. ....
10. ....
11. ....
12. ....

The Northeast: Key Chains

1. ....
2. ....
3. ....
4. ....
5. ....
6. ....
7. ....
8. ....
9. ....

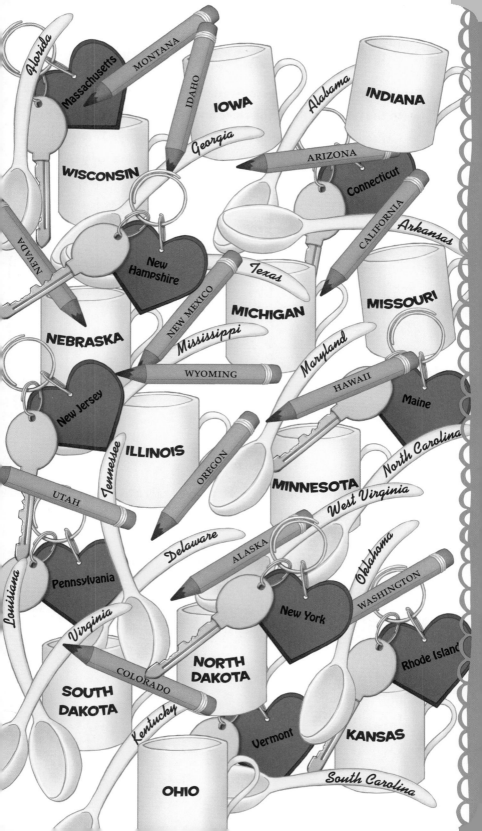

Marvelous States

Four ISU students have discovered that their home states all start with the letter M. Read the clues and use the chart to figure out who is from which state. Your US map on page 37 might come in handy, too! We've done the first one for you.

	Massachusetts	Michigan	Minnesota	Montana
Logan	no	no	yes	no
Neely			no	
Isabel			no	
Riley			no	

1. Logan is from Minnesota.

2. Neely is not from the East Coast.

3. Isabel has never seen Montana.

4. Riley's home state does not touch a large body of water.

Rhyme Time

As part of a presentation, Paige created a list of phrases that would help students learn how to pronouce the names of the Great Lakes. Match each phrase with the Great Lake name from the list.

Phrases

Pure on

Gone scary no

Wish again

Dearie

Who cheery her

Lakes

Leech

Superior

Moosehead

Yellowstone

Ontario

Mendota

Huron

Bridgeport

Erie

Louise

Wisconsin

Michigan

Did you know that the Great Lakes hold about 20 percent of the fresh water on this entire planet? That means that one-fifth of all the fresh water in the world is held in five lakes between Canada and the United States.

INNERSTAR UNIVERSITY

Great State Search

To learn all of the state capitals for her social studies class, Paige made a jumbo word search. Find the city names, listed in color below. They go forward, backward, vertically, horizontally, and diagonally.
Tip: Repeat the city and state together while you search!

Montgomery, Alabama
Juneau, Alaska
Phoenix, Arizona
Little Rock, Arkansas
Sacramento, California
Denver, Colorado
Hartford, Connecticut
Dover, Delaware
Tallahassee, Florida
Atlanta, Georgia
Honolulu, Hawaii
Boise, Idaho
Springfield, Illinois
Indianapolis, Indiana
Des Moines, Iowa
Topeka, Kansas
Frankfort, Kentucky
Baton Rouge, Louisiana
Augusta, Maine
Annapolis, Maryland
Boston, Massachusetts
Lansing, Michigan
Saint Paul, Minnesota
Jackson, Mississippi
Jefferson City, Missouri

Helena, Montana
Lincoln, Nebraska
Carson City, Nevada
Concord, New Hampshire
Trenton, New Jersey
Santa Fe, New Mexico
Albany, New York
Raleigh, North Carolina
Bismarck, North Dakota
Columbus, Ohio
Oklahoma City, Oklahoma
Salem, Oregon
Harrisburg, Pennsylvania
Providence, Rhode Island
Columbia, South Carolina
Pierre, South Dakota
Nashville, Tennessee
Austin, Texas
Salt Lake City, Utah
Montpelier, Vermont
Richmond, Virginia
Olympia, Washington
Charleston, West Virginia
Madison, Wisconsin
Cheyenne, Wyoming

Only the Facts

Logan was proofreading a friend's report on Washington, D.C. She didn't find any grammar problems, but she found six errors in fact! Read the report, and circle what you think is wrong.

Washington, D.C., is the capital of the United States. The D.C. stands for District of Columbus. Situated on the beautiful Pacific Ocean, Washington, D.C., has more than half a million residents. This state is famous for its government buildings and many landmarks, such as the Lincoln Memorial and the Space Needle. Each spring, thousands of people come to see the cherry trees and their lovely yellow blossoms. Visitors also like to tour the White House, enjoying a bit of history and hoping for a glimpse of the Queen.

Mysterious Message

Emmy was cleaning out her backpack and found a strange note
she had jotted down on an envelope. She read it and then laughed,
because she remembered why she had written it.
Can you figure out what this note is about?

HI

MA OR PA

OH OK

ME

Silly States

One day, Paige and her friends were telling each other jokes about different states. Use the key to decode the punchlines to their jokes.

1. Which state likes to draw?

P E N C I L - V A N I A

2. Which state is always under your feet?

F L O O R - I D A

3. Which state has a cold?

M A S S - A C H O O - S E T T S

4. Which state is the most curious?

W H Y - O M I N G

5. Which state is the cleanest?

W A S H I N G - T O N

6. Which state is tiny?

M I N I - S O T A

A B C D E

F G H I J

K L M N O

P Q R S T

U V W X Y

Z

State Mate

For her party, Paige created nametags in the shapes of the states in which her friends were born. Write each friend's name on her nametag. If you need help, check out the US map on page 37.

Emmy is from Oregon.
Amber is from Texas.
Shelby is from North Carolina.

Neely is from Michigan
Riley is from Montana.
Isabel is from Massachusetts.

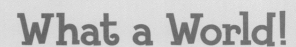

What a World!

Continental Crossword

Paige's poster of the world has spaces to write in the names of all seven continents. She's filled in all the N's and S's. Can you fill in the rest? The continents are: Asia, Africa, Europe, Australia, Antarctica, North America, and South America.

Did you know that every continent starts and ends with its same letters: North and South America, Asia, Europe, Antarctica, Africa, and Australia! See? Trivia about geography can be surprising!

Photographic Memory

Zoé, who used to live in France, pulled out photos of her first year at ISU to show Paige. Look closely at Zoé's photos for a few minutes, and then turn the page and see how many questions you can answer.

Photographic Memory

Answer these questions about the photos from the previous page.

1. Someone snapped this photo of Zoé running with Isabel. What was Zoé carrying?

_____

2. Zoé and her friends were wearing "cool" T-shirts when this photo was taken. What 1960s–1970s symbol was Zoé wearing?

_____

3. In one of the photos, Zoé was holding a purse in the air. What color was it?

_____

4. In the photo taken at the airport, how many friends were with Zoé?

_____

Polar Opposites

Shelby and Neely are working on reports for their social studies class. Read the notes each girl has written. Then use the doodles to decode the name of the region each girl is studying.

Shelby

Penguins live here.

This area is the coldest place on earth.

The south pole is located here.

- C + C + — S and K =

The _ _ _ _ _ _ _ _ _ _

Neely

Polar bears live here.

This area covers parts of Asia, North America, and Europe.

The north pole is located here.

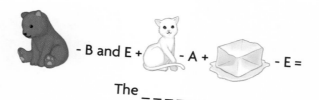

- B and E + — A + — E =

The _ _ _ _ _ _

Postcard Pile

Oh no! Paige dropped her postcard collection, and the cards scattered on the floor. Look closely at the cards for clues to match the capital cities to the correct countries. We've done the first one for you.

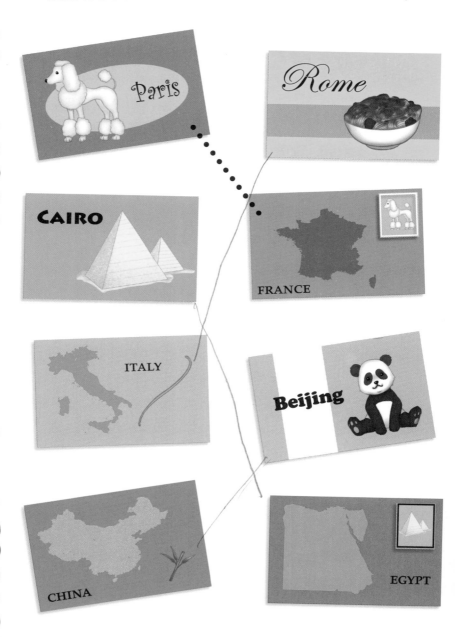

IRELAND

MEXICO CITY

AUSTRALIA

Vienna

TOKYO

Dublin

AUSTRIA

JAPAN

MEXICO

Canberra

Speaking English

Paige got a letter from her English friend, and she's having trouble understanding parts of it. Read the letter, and try to figure out what each highlighted word means and match it to its American meaning.

Dear Paige,

How is life at Innerstar U? It's been loads of fun going back to school here. I wore a new green jumper and blue trainers on my first day. During the summer while I was on holiday to visit my cousins, I had my hair cut and got fringe—lots of my school friends noticed. I'm not sure I like how it looks—what do you think? I enjoy school, and maths is my favorite subject. After school I like to play football, and then I watch the telly while having a snack of biscuits or crisps. But enough about me. Write soon and tell me about you!

Your friend,

Bridget

loads	bangs
jumper	soccer
trainers	television
holiday	cookies
fringe	sweater
maths	sneakers
football	vacation
telly	math
biscuits	potato chips
crisps	lots

Flag Fans

Shelby, Amber, Neely, and Riley are hooked on watching international soccer tournaments. Follow the twisty line from each girl to the flag of the country she's rooting for.

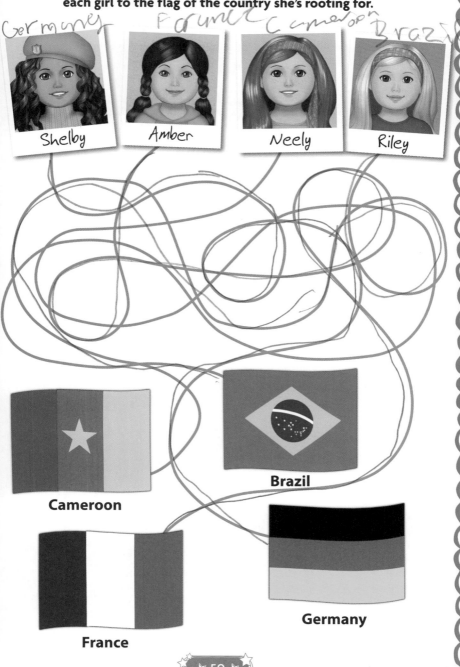

Shelby

Amber

Neely

Riley

Cameroon

Brazil

Germany

France

Big Blue World

Some of the students at Brightstar House decorated a bulletin board with photos of themselves on vacation. To figure out where they were, cross out B, L, U, and E on the frames. Then, starting at the top left edge of the frame and working your way around clockwise, write down the remaining letters in order on the blanks at right.

Photo 1

Photo 2

UELBLENULEBOE

B
L
U
E
Y
B
B

B
L
R
E
B
B
B
B

LUEABLELBUBUW

Photo 3

LUETUBLUEBUAE

B
A
U
E
B
I
B

E
B
L
N
E
B
B
Z

ELBEBNEBLUALE

Photo 4

Photo 1: ___ ___ ___ ___ ___ ___

Photo 2: ___ ___ ___ ___ ___

Photo 3: ___ ___ ___ ___ ___ ___

Photo 4: ___ ___ ___ ___ ___ ___ ___ ___

Poster Pick

Girls from Sparkle Studios designed a poster for Paige's International Week event. The artists made many versions, but Paige chose the one below. Then it got mixed in with the others! Can you find it?

1.

2.

3.

4.

5.

6.

7.

8.

9.

Collection Inspection

Isabel's grandma gave her a set of nesting dolls called a *matryoshka* (ma-TROY-shka). Put the dolls in order from the largest to smallest. Then write down the letter on each doll. If they're in the correct order, you will know what country they came from.

Where are these dolls from?

Menu Mix-ups

For International Week at ISU, the cafe and bakery are serving dishes from different countries. Look at each menu and try to unscramble the name of the country the food comes from.

TORTILLAS

CHEESE ENCHILADAS

SOPAPILLAS

XIEMOC

_____

Menu 1

Wontons

Fried Noodles

Sweet Dumplings

NICAH

_____

Menu 2

This week only! Try foods from around the world! :)

Menu 3

Tandoori Chicken

Samosas

Mango Ice Cream

A D I I N

_____

Menu 3

Menu 4

Spaetzle

Bratwurst

Apple Strudel

R Y G M E A N

_____

Menu 4

Menu 5

Lasagna

Biscotti

Gelato

L I A Y T

_____

Menu 5

People of the World

Paige is taking a quiz about the names for people from different countries. For example, people from Mexico are called Mexicans. How well would you do on her test? Draw a line from each country to the name of its people. Then check the answers to see how you scored.

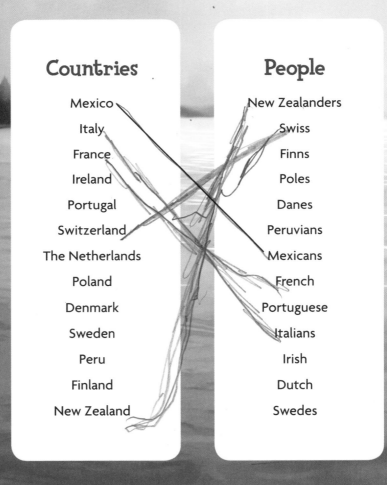

Countries	People
Mexico	New Zealanders
Italy	Swiss
France	Finns
Ireland	Poles
Portugal	Danes
Switzerland	Peruvians
The Netherlands	Mexicans
Poland	French
Denmark	Portuguese
Sweden	Italians
Peru	Irish
Finland	Dutch
New Zealand	Swedes

Places & Spaces

For geography class, Paige has to use the name of a country or a country's capital to create a new word. To help her out, fill in the blanks using the countries and capitals from her list. We've done the first one for you. Cross off each word at left as you use it.

Capitals & Countries

Bern (Switzerland)

Cuba

Lima (Peru)

~~Male~~ (Maldives)

Oman

Riga (Latvia)

Rome (Italy)

USA

New Words

1. ta _m_ _a_ _l_ _e_

2. tho __ __ __ nd

3. c __ __ __ __ te

4. s __ __ __ __

5. hi __ __ __ __ ate

6. o __ __ __ __ mi

7. ch __ __ __ __

8. w __ __ __ __

A Watery World

The girls in the Sea Life Club are working on a display. Their new poster is also a puzzle. Fill in the numbers in the boxes, and then add them to get the answer. Write the correct number in Paige's tip!

What Percentage of the Earth's Water Is in Its Oceans?

Number of US states:

+

Number of letters in the alphabet:

+

Number in a dozen:

+

Number of toes on a foot:

+

Number of seasons in a year:

=

Did you know that the Arctic Ocean is the smallest, the Atlantic is the saltiest, and the Pacific is the biggest? Our seas hold _ _ percent of the earth's water, which might explain why the world's largest animal, the blue whale, lives in the ocean!

INNERSTAR UNIVERSITY

Sounds Like . . .

Paige gave her friend Neely *Find Your Way!* and asked her to answer these questions by searching through the pages. For each page listed, fill in the first letter of the puzzle's title.

1. This European city sounds like it loves to travel.

Page   __   __   __   __
      43   46   34   38

2. This country sounds like it's sobbing.

Page   __   __   __   __   __
      36   26   19   38   30

3. This country sounds like it's cold.

Page   __   __   __   __   __
      18   22   28   19   38

4. This country sounds like something oily.

Page   __   __   __   __   __   __
      44   43   38   38   64   38

Answers

Direction Detection
Page 12
Never Eat Soggy Waffles! Starting at the top of the compass and moving around like a clock, the letters go N, E, S, W.

Busy Day
Page 13
1. Starlight Library; 2. Sparkle Studios; 3. Starfire Lake & Boathouse; 4. Real Spirit Center; 5. Star Student Center

Campus by Compass
Pages 14–15
Paige is meeting Riley at the Good Sports Center!

Symbol Search
Pages 16–17

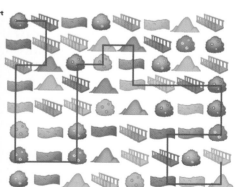

Compass Clues
Page 18
1. east; 2. north; 3. west; 4. east; 5. south; 6. north

Like a Hike?
Pages 19–21
Blue Sky Trail is the easiest because it has no steep hills, mud, or rocky paths and has fewer fallen trees than Hidden Hills Trail.

How Far?
Page 22
1. About 8½ miles; 2. About 7½ miles; 3. About 5 miles

Scavenger Hunt
Pages 23–25
The girls gave Isabel a Teddy bear. It's in her closet in a basket.

An A-maze-ing Day
Pages 26–27

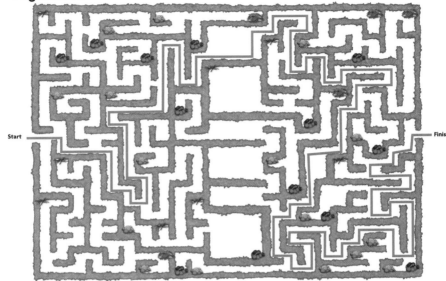

Start

Finish

Itsy-Bitsy Brainteaser
Page 28

The answer is east! The other three words appear in North Carolina, North Dakota, South Carolina, South Dakota, and West Virginia.

States with Space
Pages 30–31

Alabama, Alaska, Arizona, Arkansas, California, Colorado, Connecticut, Delaware, Florida, Georgia, Hawaii, Idaho, Illinois, Indiana, Iowa, Kansas, Kentucky, Louisiana, Maine, Maryland, Massachusetts, Michigan, Minnesota, Mississippi, Missouri, Montana, Nebraska, Nevada, New Hampshire, New Jersey, New Mexico, New York, North Carolina, North Dakota, Ohio, Oklahoma, Oregon, Pennsylvania, Rhode Island, South Carolina, South Dakota, Tennessee, Texas, Utah, Vermont, Virginia, Washington, West Virginia, Wisconsin, Wyoming

Quarter Quiz
Pages 32–33

C is Delaware; D is Kentucky; A is Nevada; B is Wyoming; F is New Jersey; G is Virginia; E is Rhode Island; H is Missouri.

Map Mistakes
Pages 34–35

- There isn't a Great Lake called "Lake Ohio." That should be the state of Ohio.
- Alaska is not connected to California.
- "Mexico" should be named New Mexico.
- There should be a border between North and South Dakota so that it's two states: North Dakota and South Dakota.
- The names for Lake Michigan and Lake Superior have been flipped.
- "New Vada" should be spelled Nevada.
- "Arkansaw" should be spelled Arkansas.
- There is no "e" at the end of "Illinois."
- "New Zealand" is not located in New York.
- The names for North Carolina and South Carolina have been flipped.
- "France" is not located in Upper Michigan.
- "Pencilvania" should be spelled Pennsylvania.
- "Marry Land" should be spelled Maryland.
- Florida does not extend below Louisiana.
- "Road Island" should be spelled Rhode Island.
- Montana's name is printed upside down.
- "Missouree" should be spelled Missouri.
- California doesn't extend beneath Arizona.
- Oklahoma's panhandle has been removed.
- "Florence" should be labeled Florida.

Extra credit: The state Paige left off her map was Hawaii!

What's In Common?
Page 36

These states all have double letters in their names. And Massachusetts, Mississippi, and Tennessee all have more than one pair of double letters.

More In Common
Page 37

These states all touch other countries. Alaska, Washington, Idaho, Montana, North Dakota, Minnesota, Michigan, New York, Vermont, New Hampshire, and Maine all touch Canada. California, Arizona, New Mexico, and Texas all touch Mexico.

Even More In Common
Page 38

These states can be drawn with straight lines. They don't have any squiggly borders at all.

Still More In Common
Page 39

Wisconsin and Michigan

Souvenir Scramble
Pages 40–41

The West: Alaska, Arizona, California, Colorado, Hawaii, Idaho, Montana, Nevada, New Mexico, Oregon, Utah, Washington, Wyoming

The South: Alabama, Arkansas, Delaware, Florida, Georgia, Kentucky, Louisiana, Maryland, Mississippi, North Carolina, Oklahoma, South Carolina, Tennessee, Texas, Virginia, West Virginia

The Midwest: Illinois, Indiana, Iowa, Kansas, Michigan, Minnesota, Missouri, Ohio, Nebraska, North Dakota, South Dakota, Wisconsin

The Northeast: Connecticut, Maine, Massachusetts, New Hampshire, New Jersey, New York, Pennsylvania, Rhode Island, Vermont

Marvelous States
Page 42

	Massachusetts	Michigan	Minnesota	Montana
Logan	no	no	yes	no
Neely	no	yes	no	no
Isabel	yes	no	no	no
Riley	no	no	no	yes

Rhyme Time
Page 43

1. Pure on = Huron
2. Gone scary no = Ontario
3. Wish again = Michigan
4. Dearie = Erie
5. Who cheery her = Superior

Great State Search
Pages 44–45

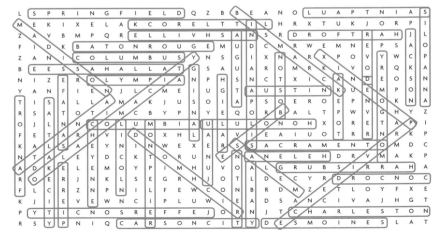

Only the Facts
Page 46

Washington, D.C., is the capital of the United States. The D.C. stands for District of
~~Columbus~~ (Columbia). Situated on the beautiful ~~Pacific Ocean~~ (East Coast on the
Potomac River), Washington, D.C., has more than half a million residents. This ~~state~~
(district—not a state) is famous for its government buildings and many landmarks,
such as the Lincoln Memorial ~~and the Space Needle.~~ (The Space Needle is in Seattle,
Washington.) Each spring, thousands of people come to see the cherry trees and
their lovely ~~yellow~~ (pink) blossoms. Visitors also like to tour the White House,
enjoying a bit of history and hoping for a glimpse of the ~~Queen.~~ (The United States
has a president.)

Mysterious Message
Page 47

These words are all postal abbreviations for states and were written down for an
upcoming test. HI: Hawaii; MA: Massachusetts; OR: Oregon; PA: Pennsylvania; OH: Ohio;
OK: Oklahoma; ME: Maine

Silly States
Pages 48–49

1. Pencil-vania; 2. Floor-ida; 3. Mass-achoo-setts; 4. Why-oming; 5. Washing-ton;
6. Mini-sota

State Mate
Page 50

Shelby

Emmy

Neely

Isabel

Amber

Riley

Continental Crossword
Page 52

Photographic Memory
Page 53–54

1. shopping bags; 2. a peace sign; 3. red; 4. three

Polar Opposites
Page 55
Shelby is studying the Antarctic, and Neely is studying the Arctic.

Speaking English
Page 58
Jumper = sweater; trainers = sneakers; holiday = vacation; fringe = bangs; maths = math; football = soccer; telly = television; biscuits = cookies; crisps = potato chips

Postcard Pile
Pages 56–57
Paris/France; Rome/Italy; Cairo/Egypt; Canberra/Australia; Vienna/Austria; Beijing/China; Dublin/Ireland; Tokyo/Japan; Mexico City/Mexico

Flag Fans
Page 59

Shelby

Amber

Neely

Riley

Big Blue World
Pages 60–61
Photo 1. Canada; Photo 2. China; Photo 3. Norway; Photo 4. Tanzania

Poster Pick
Pages 62–63
Paige likes poster 8.

Collection Inspection
Pages 64–65
The dolls are from Russia.

Menu Mix-ups
Pages 66–67
1. Mexico; 2. China;
3. India; 4. Germany; 5. Italy

People of the World
Page 68
Mexico = Mexicans; Italy = Italians; France = French; Ireland = Irish; Portugal = Portuguese; Switzerland = Swiss; The Netherlands = Dutch; Poland = Poles; Denmark = Danes; Sweden = Swedes; Peru = Peruvians; Finland = Finns; New Zealand = New Zealanders

Places & Spaces
Page 69
1. tamale; 2. thousand; 3. climate;
4. scuba; 5. hibernate; 6. origami;
7. chrome 8. woman

A Watery World
Page 70
50 + 26 + 12 + 5 + 4 = 97%

Sounds Like . . .
Page 71
1. Rome; 2. Wales; 3. Chile; 4. Greece

INNERSTARU.com

The puzzle fun continues online!

Use the code below for access to
even more puzzles and activities.

Go online to innerstarU.com/puzzle
and enter this code: FIND-WAY

Here are some other American Girl books you might like:

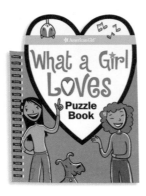

❑ I read it.

❑ I read it.

❑ I read it.

❑ I read it.

❑ I read it.

❑ I read it.

Alabama: 22nd State

Alaska: 49th State

Arizona: 48th State

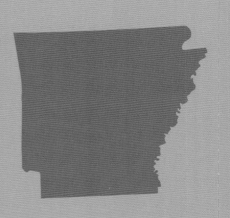

Arkansas: 25th State

California: 31st State

Colorado: 38th State

Alaska (AK)
Capital:
Juneau
State Bird:
Willow Ptarmigan
State Flower:
Forget-me-not

Alabama (AL)
Capital:
Montgomery
State Bird:
Yellowhammer
State Flower:
Camellia

Arkansas (AR)
Capital:
Little Rock
State Bird:
Mockingbird
State Flower:
Apple Blossom

Arizona (AZ)
Capital:
Phoenix
State Bird:
Cactus Wren
State Flower:
Saguaro Cactus Blossom

Colorado (CO)
Capital:
Denver
State Bird:
Lark Bunting
State Flower:
Rocky Mountain Columbine

California (CA)
Capital:
Sacramento
State Bird:
California Valley Quail
State Flower:
California Poppy

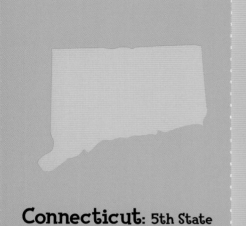

Connecticut: 5th State

Delaware: 1st State

Florida: 27th State

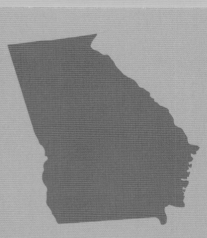

Georgia: 4th State

Hawaii: 50th State

Idaho: 43rd State

Delaware (DE)
Capital:
Dover
State Bird:
Blue Hen Chicken
State Flower:
Peach Blossom

Connecticut (CT)
Capital:
Hartford
State Bird:
Robin
State Flower:
Mountain Laurel

Georgia (GA)
Capital:
Atlanta
State Bird:
Brown Thrasher
State Flower:
Cherokee Rose

Florida (FL)
Capital:
Tallahassee
State Bird:
Mockingbird
State Flower:
Orange Blossom

Idaho (ID)
Capital:
Boise
State Bird:
Mountain Bluebird
State Flower:
Syringa

Hawaii (HI)
Capital:
Honolulu
State Bird:
Nene
State Flower:
Yellow Hibiscus

Illinois: 21st State

Indiana: 19th State

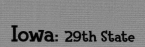

Iowa: 29th State

Kansas: 34th State

Kentucky: 15th State

Louisiana: 18th State

Indiana (IN)
Capital:
Indianapolis
State Bird:
Cardinal
State Flower:
Peony

Illinois (IL)
Capital:
Springfield
State Bird:
Cardinal
State Flower:
Purple Violet

Kansas (KS)
Capital:
Topeka
State Bird:
Western Meadowlark
State Flower:
Sunflower

Iowa (IA)
Capital:
Des Moines
State Bird:
Eastern Goldfinch
State Flower:
Wild Prairie Rose

Louisiana (LA)
Capital:
Baton Rouge
State Bird:
Eastern Brown Pelican
State Flower:
Magnolia

Kentucky (KY)
Capital:
Frankfort
State Bird:
Cardinal
State Flower:
Goldenrod

Maine: 23rd State

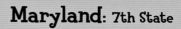

Maryland: 7th State

Massachusetts: 6th State

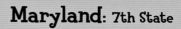

Michigan: 26th State

Minnesota: 32nd State

Mississippi: 20th State

Maryland (MD)
Capital:
Annapolis
State Bird:
Baltimore Oriole
State Flower:
Black-Eyed Susan

Maine (ME)
Capital:
Augusta
State Bird:
Chickadee
State Flower:
White Pine Cone and Tassel

Michigan (MI)
Capital:
Lansing
State Bird:
Robin
State Flower:
Apple Blossom

Massachusetts (MA)
Capital:
Boston
State Bird:
Chickadee
State Flower:
Mayflower

Mississippi (MS)
Capital:
Jackson
State Bird:
Mockingbird
State Flower:
Magnolia

Minnesota (MN)
Capital:
St. Paul
State Bird:
Common Loon
State Flower:
Pink and White Lady's Slipper

Missouri: 24th State

Montana: 41st State

Nebraska: 37th State

Nevada: 36th State

New Hampshire: 9th State

New Jersey: 3rd State

Montana (MT)
Capital:
Helena
State Bird:
Western Meadowlark
State Flower:
Bitterroot

Missouri (MO)
Capital:
Jefferson City
State Bird:
Bluebird
State Flower:
White Hawthorn Blossom

Nevada (NV)
Capital:
Carson City
State Bird:
Mountain Bluebird
State Flower:
Sagebrush

Nebraska (NE)
Capital:
Lincoln
State Bird:
Western Meadowlark
State Flower:
Goldenrod

New Jersey (NJ)
Capital:
Trenton
State Bird:
Eastern Goldfinch
State Flower:
Violet

New Hampshire (NH)
Capital:
Concord
State Bird:
Purple Finch
State Flower:
Purple Lilac

New York: 11th State

New Mexico: 47th State

North Carolina:
12th State

North Dakota:
39th State

Ohio: 17th State

Oklahoma: 46th State

New Mexico (NM)
Capital:
Santa Fe
State Bird:
Roadrunner
State Flower:
Yucca Flower

New York (NY)
Capital:
Albany
State Bird:
Bluebird
State Flower:
Rose

North Dakota (ND)
Capital:
Bismarck
State Bird:
Western Meadowlark
State Flower:
Wild Prairie Rose

North Carolina (NC)
Capital:
Raleigh
State Bird:
Cardinal
State Flower:
Flowering Dogwood

Oklahoma (OK)
Capital:
Oklahoma City
State Bird:
Scissor-Tailed Flycatcher
State Flower:
Oklahoma Rose

Ohio (OH)
Capital:
Columbus
State Bird:
Cardinal
State Flower:
Scarlet Carnation

Oregon: 33rd State

Pennsylvania: 2nd State

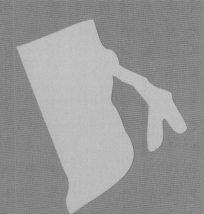

Rhode Island:
13th State

South Carolina:
8th State

South Dakota:
40th State

Tennessee: 16th State

Pennsylvania (PA)

Capital:
Harrisburg

State Bird:
Ruffed Grouse

State Flower:
Mountain Laurel

Oregon (OR)

Capital:
Salem

State Bird:
Western Meadowlark

State Flower:
Oregon Grape

South Carolina (SC)

Capital:
Columbia

State Bird:
Great Carolina Wren

State Flower:
Yellow Jessamine

Rhode Island (RI)

Capital:
Providence

State Bird:
Rhode Island Red

State Flower:
Violet

Tennessee (TN)

Capital:
Nashville

State Bird:
Mockingbird

State Flower:
Iris

South Dakota (SD)

Capital:
Pierre

State Bird:
Ring-Necked Pheasant

State Flower:
Pasque Flower

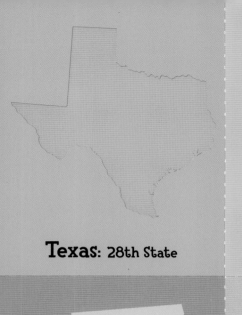

Texas: 28th State

Utah: 45th State

Vermont: 14th State

Virginia: 10th State

Washington: 42nd State

West Virginia: 35th State

Utah (UT)
Capital:
Salt Lake City
State Bird:
California Seagull
State Flower:
Sego Lily

Texas (TX)
Capital:
Austin
State Bird:
Mockingbird
State Flower:
Bluebonnet

Virginia (VA)
Capital:
Richmond
State Bird:
Cardinal
State Flower:
American Dogwood

Vermont (VT)
Capital:
Montpelier
State Bird:
Hermit Thrush
State Flower:
Red Clover

West Virginia (WV)
Capital:
Charleston
State Bird:
Cardinal
State Flower:
Rhododendron

Washington (WA)
Capital:
Olympia
State Bird:
Willow Goldfinch
State Flower:
Coast Rhododendron

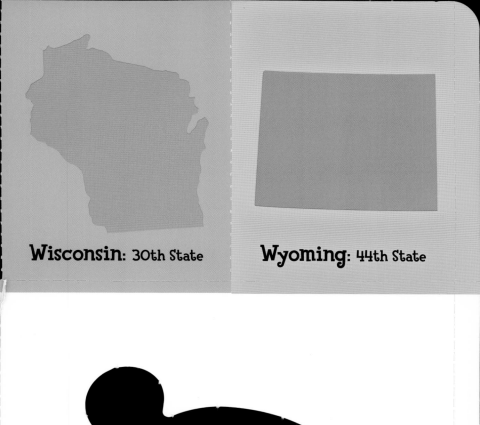

Wisconsin: 30th State

Wyoming: 44th State

Wyoming (WY)

Capital:

Cheyenne

State Bird:

Western Meadowlark

State Flower:

Indian Paintbrush

Wisconsin (WI)

Capital:

Madison

State Bird:

Robin

State Flower:

Wood Violet